HOLIDAY ORIGAMI

St. Patrick's Day Origami

by Ruth Owen

PowerKiDS
press™

New York

Published in 2015 by
The Rosen Publishing Group, Inc.
29 East 21st Street, New York, NY 10010

Library of Congress Cataloging-in-Publication Data
Owen, Ruth.
St. Patrick's Day origami / by Ruth Owen.
p. cm. — (Holiday origami)
Includes index.
ISBN 978-1-4777-5719-2 (pbk.)
ISBN 978-1-4777-5720-8 (6-pack)
ISBN 978-1-4777-5718-5 (library binding)
1. Origami — Juvenile literature. 2. Saint Patrick's Day decorations — Juvenile literature.
I. Owen, Ruth, 1967-. II. Title.
TT900.S25 O94 2015
736/.982—d23

Produced for Rosen by Ruby Tuesday Books Ltd
Editor for Ruby Tuesday Books Ltd: Mark J. Sachner
US Editor: Sara Antill
Designer: Emma Randall

Photo Credits: Cover, 1, 3, 5, 7, 8, 12, 16 (Stuart Monk), 20, 24, 28 © Shutterstock.

Origami models © Ruby Tuesday Books Ltd.

Manufactured in the United States of America
CPSIA Compliance Information: Batch # CW15PK: For Further Information contact Rosen Publishing, New York, New York at 1-800-237-9932

Contents

Origami in Action

St. Patrick's Day is a religious celebration that is held on March 17th every year. It **commemorates** the death of St. Patrick, the patron saint of Ireland. This special day is a huge celebration in Ireland and in other parts of the world where Irish people have settled.

This year, you can get ready for St. Patrick's Day by making fun decorations using **origami**, the art of folding paper. No one knows where origami got started, but it has been popular for centuries in Japan. In fact, "origami" is Japanese for "folding paper."

If you've never tried origami before, don't be nervous. Just follow the step-by-step instructions and you'll soon be folding paper shamrocks and leprechauns!

Get Folding!

Before you get started on your St. Patrick's Day origami models, here are some tips.

Tip 1

Read all the instructions carefully and look at the pictures. Make sure you understand what's required before you begin a fold. Don't rush; be patient. Work slowly and carefully.

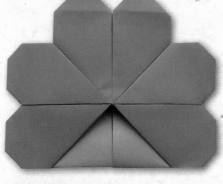

Tip 2

Folding a piece of paper sounds easy, but it can be tricky to get neat, accurate folds. The more you practice, the easier it becomes.

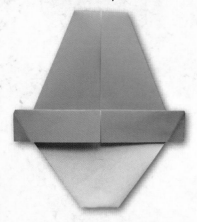

Tip 3

If an instruction says "crease," make the crease as flat as possible. The flatter the creases, the better the model. You can make a sharp crease by running a plastic ruler along the edge of the paper.

Tip 4

Sometimes, at first, your models may look a little crumpled. Don't give up! The more models you make, the better you will get at folding and creasing.

When it comes to origami, practice makes perfect!

Origami is a very popular hobby. People of all ages love making paper models. Some people are such experts, they can make very complicated models like those on this page.

All these models were made just by folding paper. Keep practicing and you could soon become an origami master.

Some origami models are made from hundreds of small sections, or modules.

Origami Celtic Cross

St. Patrick was born in Britain during the 4th century. He became a priest and traveled to Ireland. Here, he spread the Christian religion and converted many Irish people to Christianity. Before St. Patrick came to Ireland, people believed in **pagan** religions. They celebrated nature and worshipped the sun.

One of the **symbols** that is often associated with St. Patrick's Day is the **Celtic** cross. **Legends** say that St. Patrick combined the Christian cross with the sun to create a religious symbol that celebrated both nature and God the creator.

Celtic crosses come in many designs, and this first project shows you how to make a mini-origami paper cross.

To make a Celtic cross, you will need:

One sheet of origami paper in your choice of color

Scissors   Glue

(Origami paper is sometimes colored on both sides or white on one side.)

STEP 1:

Cut the sheet of paper in half and work with one half. This paper is green on one side and yellow on the other. We want to make a green cross, so we placed the paper green-side down.

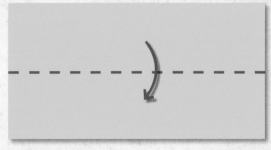

Fold the paper in half, crease well, and unfold.

STEP 2:

Now fold the top and the bottom halves of the paper into the center, and crease.

STEP 3:

Fold the right-hand side of the model over to the left along the dotted line, and crease hard. Then fold the right-hand side back again, making a small pleat.

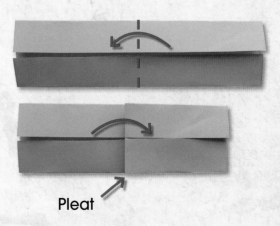

Pleat

9

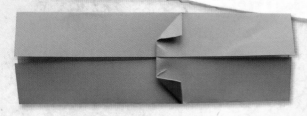

STEP 4:
Fold in the two points in the center of the model, and crease hard.

STEP 5:
Fold the bottom right-hand edge of the model up and into the center. As you do this, the folded point should open out. As it does, squash it flat to form a triangle.

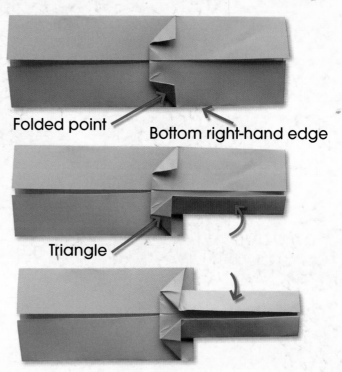

Folded point

Bottom right-hand edge

Triangle

Repeat on the top right-hand side of the model.

STEP 6:
Now fold the left-hand side of the model over to the right along the dotted line, and crease. Then fold the left-hand side back again, making a small pleat.

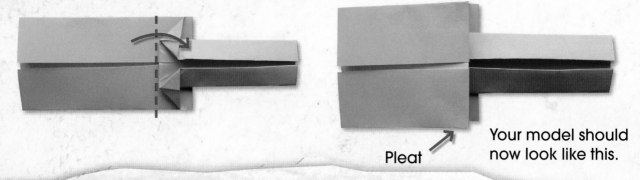

Pleat

Your model should now look like this.

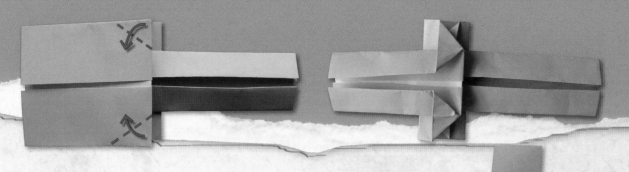

STEP 7:

Fold in the two points in the center of the model, and crease hard.

Then repeat what you did in Step 5 on the left-hand side of your model.

STEP 8:

To make the sun-like center section of the cross, take the other half of the piece of paper and cut it in half so you now have a quarter-sized piece. Fold the paper into four quarters. Then fold each corner into the center of the model, creasing hard.

Turn your model over, and it will look like this.

STEP 9:

Turn the model over and fold the four corners into the center again, creasing hard.

STEP 10:

Turn the model over again, and fold the four corners into the center, creasing hard.

STEP 11:

Finally, turn the model over one more time. Fold each corner behind to create a rounded shape. Then glue the Sun to the center of the cross.

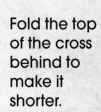

Fold the top of the cross behind to make it shorter.

Origami Shamrock

Another symbol that's associated with St. Patrick's Day is the three-leaf shamrock. Legend says that St. Patrick used the leaves of this tiny green plant to explain the holy trinity to the Irish people. He used the shamrock as a symbol of the Father, the Son, and the Holy Spirit.

Today, the shamrock is a symbol of Ireland, and is a popular decoration on St. Patrick's Day.

To make a shamrock, you will need:

Four sheets of green paper

Glue or tape

(Origami paper is sometimes colored on both sides or white on one side.)

STEP 1:

The shamrock is made from three modules, or sections. To make one module, place the paper green-side down. Fold the paper in half from side to side, crease, and unfold. Then fold in half from top to bottom, crease, and unfold.

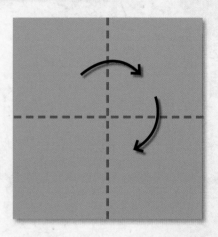

STEP 2:

Fold down the top half of the paper so it meets the center, and crease. Then turn the paper over.

STEP 3:

Now fold down the two top corners into the center of the model, and crease well.

STEP 4:

Turn the model over, and it should look like this.

Now fold down the top of the model so it meets the bottom, and crease well.

STEP 5:

Turn the model over again. Now lift up the small rectangular flap on the left-hand side. As you lift up the flap, you will see a small triangle forming. Gently flatten this triangle.

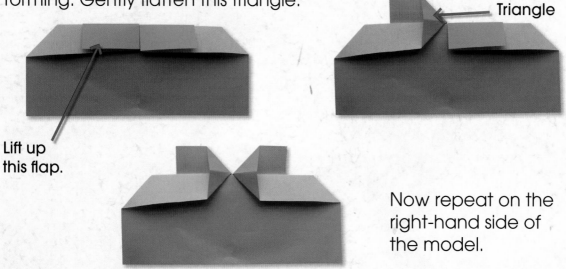

Triangle

Lift up
this flap.

Now repeat on the right-hand side of the model.

STEP 6:

Fold in the sides of the model along the dotted lines, and crease hard.

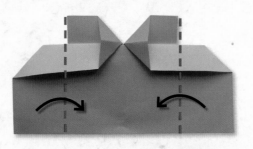

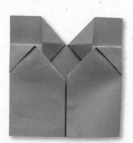

STEP 7:
Fold in the two top corners of the model along the dotted lines, and crease.

STEP 8:
Now fold down the two top points of the model, and crease.

STEP 9:
Turn the model over and your first module is complete. Now repeat Steps 1 to 8 two more times so you have three heart-shaped modules in total.

STEP 10:
To join the modules together, slide the pale green triangle of one module under the dark green heart of another. Glue or tape the modules together.

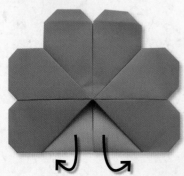

STEP 11:
When all three modules are joined, fold the remaining two bottom triangles behind the model.

STEP 12:
Finally, fold or roll up a small piece of green paper to make a stalk, and tape or glue it behind the shamrock leaves.

Origami Leprechaun

When St. Patrick's Day comes around, you might see people wearing big green hats and even green suits. That's because they are dressed as creatures called leprechauns. Irish legends include many tales of leprechauns and other fairy folk.

Leprechauns are said to look like tiny men with orange or red beards and green suits. They collect money and gold, and hide it away.

This next project shows you how to make a paper leprechaun using origami and some cutting and gluing.

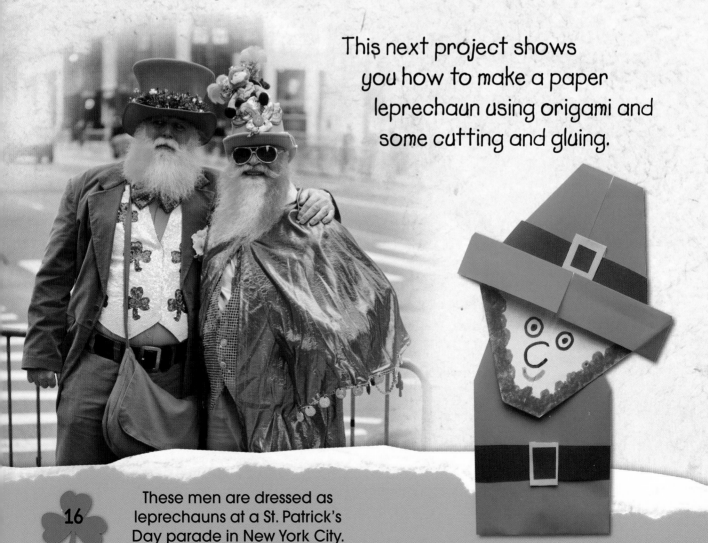

These men are dressed as leprechauns at a St. Patrick's Day parade in New York City.

To make a leprechaun, you will need:

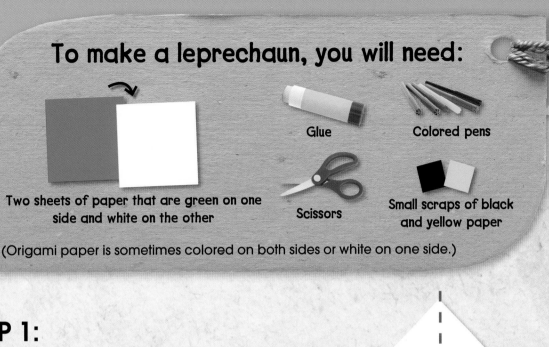

Two sheets of paper that are green on one side and white on the other

Glue

Colored pens

Scissors

Small scraps of black and yellow paper

(Origami paper is sometimes colored on both sides or white on one side.)

STEP 1:
To make the leprechaun's head, place the paper colored-side down. Fold the paper in half diagonally, crease, and unfold.

STEP 2:
Now fold in the two sides of the model so they meet in the center, and crease well.

STEP 3:
Fold up the bottom half of the model along the dotted line, and crease.

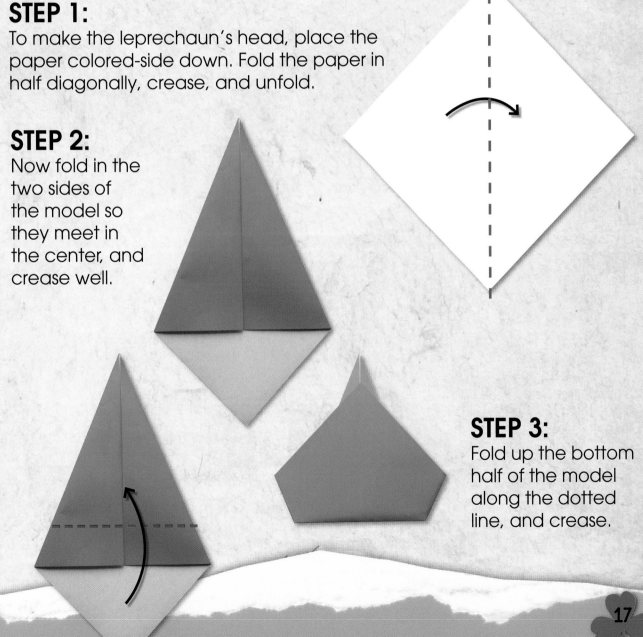

STEP 4:

Now fold the top layer of paper back down along the dotted line, and crease.

Your model should now look like this.

STEP 5:

Fold in the sides of the model along the dotted lines, and crease well.

Square edge

STEP 6:

The folds you made in Step 5 will have created two tiny pockets at points A and B. Gently open out these pockets, and then squash them flat to create a square edge.

Your model should look like this.

STEP 7:

Fold down the top point of the model and fold up the bottom point. Crease well.

STEP 8:

To make the leprechaun's body, repeat Steps 1 and 2 with the second piece of paper. Then fold up the bottom of the model, and crease.

Turn the model over, and the leprechaun's head is complete.

STEP 9:

Now fold down the top point of the model so it overlaps the bottom point, and crease well.

STEP 10:

Fold in the sides of the model along the dotted lines, and crease. The sides will now allow your leprechaun model to stand up.

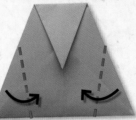

STEP 11:

Now slide the body into the back of the head. You can use a little glue or tape to hold it in place.

STEP 12:

Turn the model over. To decorate the leprechaun, draw on a face and beard. Glue on small pieces of black and yellow paper to decorate the hat and make a belt.

Origami Pot of Gold

Old Irish legends say that if you capture a leprechaun and keep your eye on him, the little creature won't be able to vanish. In order to win his freedom, the leprechaun will tell you where his pot of gold is hidden.

Follow the instructions in this next project to make a cute little pot, or box. Fill it with yellow candy or cereal, and you will have your own pot of gold for your St. Patrick's Day celebrations.

To make a pot of gold, you will need:

One sheet of paper in your
choice of color

Small pieces of yellow
candy or cereal

(Origami paper is sometimes colored on both sides or white on one side.)

STEP 1:

Begin by placing the paper
with the color of your pot
facing up. We chose to
make a dark green pot
with pale green inside. Fold
the paper diagonally from
side to side, crease, and
unfold. Then fold from top to
bottom, crease, and unfold.

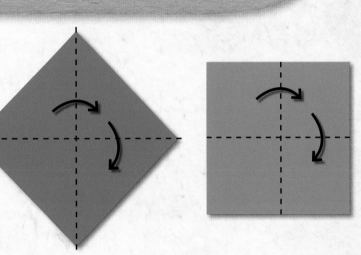

Turn the paper over. Fold the paper from
side to side, crease, and unfold. Then fold
from top to bottom, crease, and unfold.

STEP 2:

Now fold and close up the paper by bringing points
A and B to meet each other, and point C down
to meet point D.

Your flattened
model should
now look like this.

STEP 3:

Working with the top layer of paper only, fold the right-hand side of the model into the center, and crease well.

Then open out the fold you've just made, and squash it flat to create a kite shape.

Repeat on the left-hand side of the model.

STEP 4:

Turn the model over and repeat Step 3 on the other side. Your model should now look like this.

STEP 5:

Now, pick up your model, and you will see that it has four sides, or faces. Two will have kite shapes, and two will be flat. Adjust the model so that there is a flat face on top and on the bottom, and lay the model down again. Your model should look like this.

Now, working only with the top layer of paper, fold the right-hand side of the model into the center, and crease.

Repeat on the left-hand side.

Turn the model over and fold the sides into the center, creasing well.

Crease

STEP 6:
Now fold up the bottom point of the model so it meets the top point, crease hard, and unfold.

STEP 7:
Now take hold of the bottom points of the model and gently pull them apart. You will see that the top half of the model is forming the box shape.

This next part is tricky, but slide your fingers inside the model and carefully press out and shape the box until it looks like this.

Fill your box with yellow candy or cereal, and your St. Patrick's Day pot of gold is complete!

Origami Rainbow

Would a leprechaun really reveal the hiding place of his precious gold? Legend says that crafty leprechauns will not give up their gold that easily, and will play tricks on humans. Old tales say that a leprechaun might say his gold is hidden at the end of a rainbow. Of course, everyone knows it's not possible to find the end of a rainbow!

Complete your St. Patrick's Day leprechaun story by making this colorful origami rainbow to go with your paper leprechaun and pot of gold.

To make a rainbow, you will need:

Seven sheets of origami paper in rainbow colors (red, orange, yellow, green, blue, indigo, and violet)

Glue or tape

(Origami paper is sometimes colored on both sides or white on one side.)

STEP 1:

We made a rainbow with seven sections, or modules. To make one module, place a piece of paper colored-side down. Fold it in half from side to side, crease, and unfold. Then fold from top to bottom, crease, and unfold.

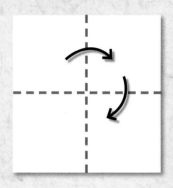

STEP 2:

Fold the top two corners of the paper into the center creases, and crease well.

STEP 3:

Fold up the bottom half of the model to meet the center crease, then crease, and unfold.

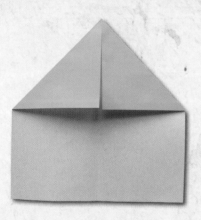

STEP 4:

Now fold up the bottom of the model along the red dotted line, and crease.

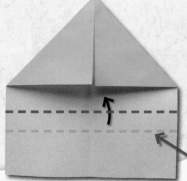

Crease made in Step 3.

25

STEP 5:

Turn the model over. Fold in the two small triangles on the sides of the model.

STEP 6:

Fold up the bottom of the model along the dotted line, tucking the two small triangles inside. Crease well.

STEP 7:

Now fold the model in half along the dotted line by folding the right-hand side of the model behind. This first module is now complete.

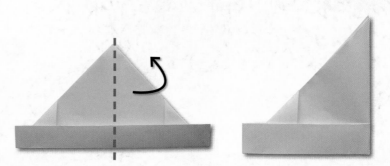

STEP 8:

Repeat Steps 1 to 7 to make the remaining six modules.

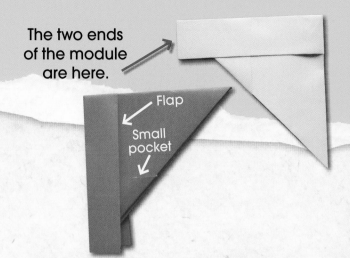

The two ends of the module are here.

Flap

Small pocket

STEP 9:

To join the modules together, take two modules and position them as shown. You will see there is a flap and small pocket on the left-hand side of the red module.

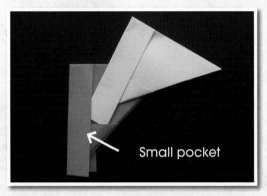

Small pocket

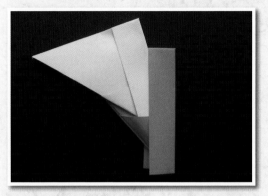

Now slide the orange module over the top of the red module so that the red module is between the two ends of the orange module. Slide one end of the orange module into the flap and pocket on the front of the red module. Slide the other end section into the flap and pocket on the back of the red module.

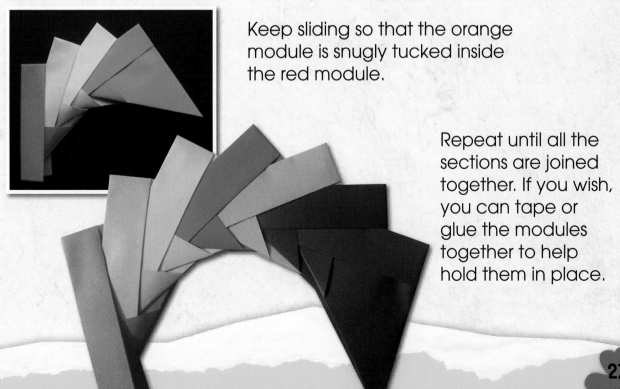

Keep sliding so that the orange module is snugly tucked inside the red module.

Repeat until all the sections are joined together. If you wish, you can tape or glue the modules together to help hold them in place.

Origami Ribbon

You've probably noticed that the color green features a lot on St. Patrick's Day. That's because green is an important color for Ireland. The color green appears on Ireland's flag and is also the country's national color.

Ireland is often called "the Emerald Isle" because of its grassy, rolling hills and green fields. People say that Ireland's landscape has 40 shades of green.

In this final project, make a green St. Patrick's Day ribbon to wear during your celebrations. Have fun making your ribbon, and have a great St. Patrick's Day.

To make a ribbon, you will need:

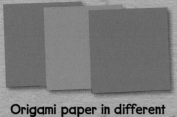

Origami paper in different shades of green

Glue

scissors

A piece of thin cardboard measuring about 4 inches square (10 sq cm)

A pen

Tape

A safety pin

(Origami paper is sometimes colored on both sides or white on one side.)

STEP 1:

To make a ribbon that measures about 4 inches (10 cm) across, you will need 12 pieces of paper each measuring 3 inches by 2 inches (7.5 cm x 5 cm).

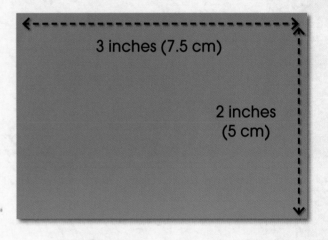

3 inches (7.5 cm)

2 inches (5 cm)

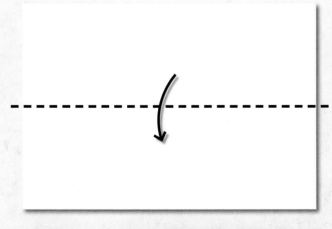

STEP 2:

To make one module of the ribbon, place a piece of paper colored-side down, fold it in half along the dotted line, and crease hard. Now fold the model in half again along the dotted line, crease, and then unfold.

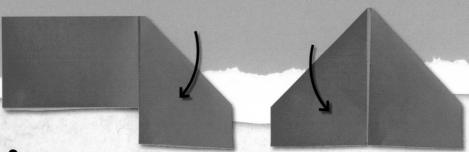

STEP 3:

Fold down the right-hand side of the model to meet the center crease you've just made, and crease hard. Then repeat on the left-hand side.

STEP 4:

Turn the model over. Fold up the two bottom corners, and crease.

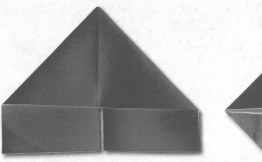

STEP 5:

Fold up the two flaps at the bottom of the model, and crease. You should now have a triangle.

STEP 6:

Fold the triangle in half. On the left-hand edge of the model, you will now have two pockets. On the lower right-hand side, you will have two points. This is one module of the ribbon.

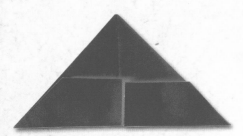

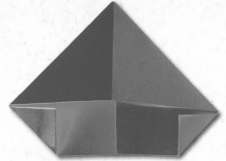

Pockets in here

Two points here

STEP 7:

Repeat Steps 2 to 6 to make 11 more modules, or triangles.

STEP 8:
To begin constructing the ribbon, slot the two points of one triangle into the two pockets of another triangle.

STEP 9:
Finally, when all the triangles are slotted together, slide the two points of triangle 12 into the pockets of triangle 1 to complete the "circle."

STEP 10:
Cut a rough circle from your piece of cardboard. Write on your St. Patrick's Day message. Next, glue the origami circle onto the cardboard. Cut two long strips of paper and glue them to the back. Tape on a safety pin and wear your origami ribbon with pride!

Glossary

Celtic (KEL-tik) Related to or having to do with the religions, languages, and cultures of people and tribes who lived in parts of modern-day Europe.

commemorates (cuh-MEH-muh-rayts) Remembers a person or event with a special ceremony or celebration.

legends (LEJ-uhndz) Stories handed down from long ago that are often based on some facts but cannot be proven to be true.

origami (or-uh-GAH-mee) The art of folding paper into decorative shapes or objects.

pagan (PAY-gun) Relating to people from the past who followed religions that often had more than one god and were strongly connected to nature. Some pagans worshipped the Sun.

symbols (SIM-bulz) Objects or pictures that stand for or represent another thing, such as an important event or person. For example, a cross may be a symbol of Christianity.

Index

Websites

Due to the changing nature of Internet links, PowerKids Press has developed an online list of websites related to the subject of this book. This site is updated regularly. Please use this link to access the list:
www.powerkidslinks.com/ho/stpat